10-Minute Crafts

EASTER CRAFTS

ANNALEES LIM

WINDMILL
BOOKS
New York

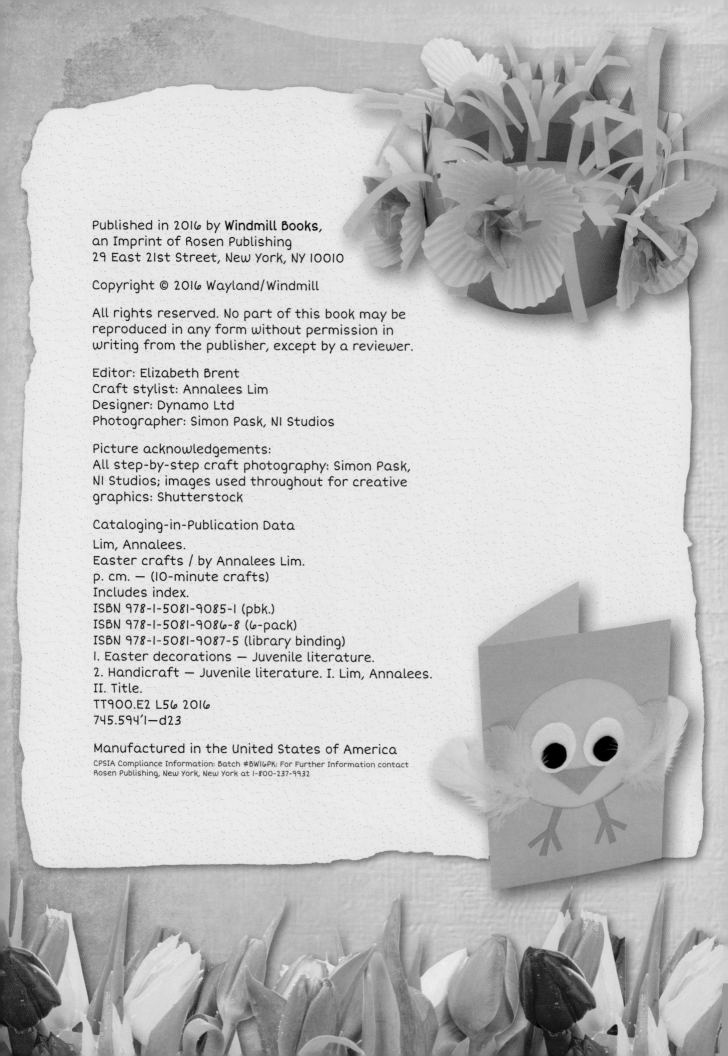

Published in 2016 by **Windmill Books**,
an Imprint of Rosen Publishing
29 East 21st Street, New York, NY 10010

Editor: Elizabeth Brent
Craft stylist: Annalees Lim
Designer: Dynamo Ltd
Photographer: Simon Pask, NI Studios

Picture acknowledgements:
All step-by-step craft photography: Simon Pask,
NI Studios; images used throughout for creative
graphics: Shutterstock

Cataloging-in-Publication Data
Lim, Annalees.
Easter crafts / by Annalees Lim.
p. cm. — (10-minute crafts)
Includes index.
ISBN 978-1-5081-9085-1 (pbk.)
ISBN 978-1-5081-9086-8 (6-pack)
ISBN 978-1-5081-9087-5 (library binding)
1. Easter decorations — Juvenile literature.
2. Handicraft — Juvenile literature. I. Lim, Annalees.
II. Title.
TT900.E2 L56 2016
745.594'1—d23

Manufactured in the United States of America
CPSIA Compliance Information: Batch #BW16PK: For Further Information contact
Rosen Publishing, New York, New York at 1-800-237-9932

Contents

Easter

Easter is a celebration of new life and rebirth, and people celebrate this holiday in many different ways. In this book you will find simple crafts to help make your Easter festivities really fun. Each project will take you only about 10 minutes to make, so you will still have plenty of time to go in search of tasty treats on an Easter egg hunt!

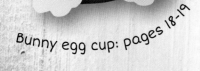

Bunny egg cup: pages 18-19

All of these projects use different papers, from tissue paper to card stock, and paper plates. Before you go out and buy supplies, have a look at what you have at home. There are lots of things that can be recycled, such as old Easter cards, which are great for cutting out flowers to decorate the Easter bunny picture on pages 14-15, candy wrappers and foils to use as decorations, leftover ribbons from packaging, or old envelopes to use as scrap paper. Whatever you find, store it away in a craft bag or box, ready for the next time you get creative.

Crafting can be messy, especially if you are using glitter or glue, so make sure you cover all your work surfaces with old newspaper or a plastic tablecloth before you begin. Always wash your hands after you have used glue to keep your works of art from being ruined by sticky fingers, and always ask an adult to help you with scissors or sharp compasses.

Crêpe paper chicken hanging: pages 22-23

Easter basket: pages 8-9

So with Easter fast approaching, take some time to get messy with these crafts to decorate and celebrate this time of year.

A note about measurements

Measurements are given in U.S. form with metric in parentheses. The metric conversion is rounded to make it easier to measure.

Flower bonnet

Parade around with pride in this beautiful bonnet, which is covered in delicate daffodils.

You will need:

- Green card stock
- A fabric tape measure
- Scissors
- A stapler
- Yellow cupcake cups
- Green and orange tissue paper
- A glue stick
- A ruler

1

Measure around your head using the tape measure, then cut a piece of green card stock the same length, and 4 inches (10 cm) wide. You may have to staple two lengths of card together.

2

Cut triangle shapes out of the top to make it look like grass, and then staple the ends together to make a headband.

Fold one of the cupcake cups into quarters and round off the top. Open it up and it will make four petals. Glue on some rolled-up orange tissue paper to make the center of the flower.

Make five daffodils and glue them onto the green headband.

Cut a 4-inch-wide (10 cm) piece of tissue paper to the same length as your headband. Cut slits into the top and glue it to the inside of the headband so the cut bits stick out over the top.

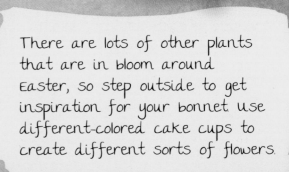

There are lots of other plants that are in bloom around Easter, so step outside to get inspiration for your bonnet use different-colored cake cups to create different sorts of flowers.

Easter basket

Make this colorful Easter egg-shaped basket to collect all your chocolatey treats in when you are on an egg hunt.

You will need:

- Two colored bowls made from paper, thin plastic, or styrofoam
- Scissors
- A stapler
- Yellow card stock
- A ruler
- Ribbon
- Craft glue
- Sticky dots

1

Cut out some triangles from one side of each bowl to make it look like a cracked egg.

2

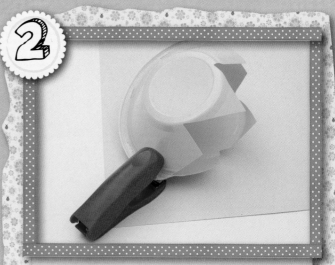

Put the two bowls together and staple around the edge to make the main basket shape.

3

Cut out a 1-by-12-inch (2.5 x 30 cm) strip from the yellow stock and staple it onto the basket to make a handle.

4

Make two bows from the ribbon and glue them onto the handle to cover the staples.

5

Stick lots of colorful sticky dots all over the basket.

Make more baskets from white paper bowls and staple some card stock ears onto the top to turn them into bunnies! Remember to draw a face on the front You could even stick a white pom-pom tail to the back too.

Felt chick card

People will love receiving this Easter card. It feels furry and feathery, like a real chick.

1

Fold the blue card stock in half, and then fold one of the halves in half again.

2

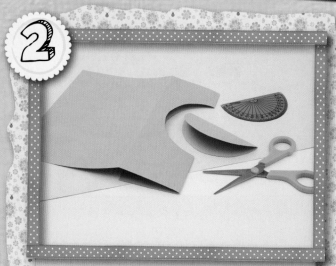

Draw a small semicircle onto the second folded section, and cut it out to make a circle.

3

Cut out a piece of yellow felt that is slightly bigger than the circle and stick it to the back of the circle-shaped hole using some craft glue.

4

Make some eyes from the black and white felt and stick them onto the body, then use more craft glue to stick yellow feathers to either side of the felt circle.

5

Cut out a triangle beak and some feet from the orange paper and stick them onto the card.

Use different colors of felt to turn your cards into other animals, such as sheep or bunnies.

Easter bunny picture

Make the cute Easter bunnies bounce and skip over the hills in this fun spinning picture.

1

Draw around the plate onto the green and blue card stock and cut out the shapes so you have two circles that are identical in size.

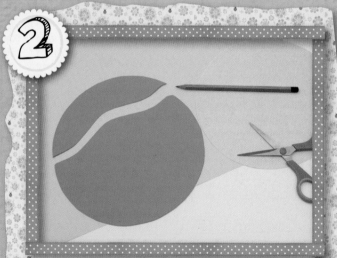

2

Cut a wavy line off the top of the green circle.

Cut six bunny shapes out of the white paper and stick them onto the edge of the blue circle.

Go around the bunny shapes in black pen. Draw ears, legs, and a tail onto each bunny shape and color the ears in pink too.

Place the green circle on top of the blue circle and press a paper fastener into the middle to hold them together. Decorate the green hills with yellow paper flowers.

Spin the blue circle to make it look as if the bunnies are bouncing over the hills. You could also make a spinning picture to show sheep leaping over a flowery meadow or birds flying through the sky

Seasonal sparkling mobile

Easter happens at about the same time every year but you never know what the weather will be like. Make this raindrop mobile to hang inside to keep the rain away outside.

You will need:

- White card stock, 8½ by 11 inch (21.5 × 28 cm)
- A black felt-tipped pen
- Scissors
- A hole punch
- Silver thread
- A ruler
- Cotton balls
- A glue stick
- Silver card stock

1

Fold the white card stock in half, and draw a cloud shape on one side. Cut this out, and make one hole at the top and five holes at the bottom using the hole punch.

2

Tie a loop of silver thread to the top of the cloud and five 12-inch (30 cm) pieces of thread to the bottom of the cloud.

3

Glue cotton balls onto the front and back of the cloud using the glue stick.

4

Cut out 26 matching raindrop shapes from the silver card stock.

5

Glue a pair of raindrops around a silver thread. Repeat until you have glued all of the raindrops onto all five threads.

You can add more things to your mobile. Try gray storm clouds, a rainbow or even a pair of shiny rain boots.

Bunny egg cup

Make this cute bunny decoration to show off your chocolate treats. They will look so good, you won't be able to resist eating them for long!

You will need:
- A foil-wrapped Easter egg
- An old egg cup
- White card stock
- A ruler
- Scissors
- Pink card stock
- A glue stick
- Googly eyes
- A black felt-tipped pen
- Sticky tack

Make a headband for the egg using a small, $3/8$-inch-wide (1 cm) strip of card stock. Stick two bunny ears, made of white card stock and pink card stock, to the top of the band.

Stick two googly eyes onto the headband.

Cut out a heart shape from the pink card stock and draw a nose onto it. Cut out some white teeth and stick them to the back of the heart.

Glue the nose and teeth onto the headband.

Make two sets of paws out of the white card stock. Tuck the front paws into the egg cup and use sticky tack to stick the back paws onto the base of the egg cup.

Ask an adult to help you remove the inside of a real egg. Do this by making two small holes in the shell, and blowing out the contents. Then you can paint the eggshell and it will last year after year.

Easter egg pin badge

This clay badge is great to wear during Easter celebrations. It is so simple to make that you will want to make one for all your friends and family too.

1

Roll out some clay so that it is 1/4 inch (0.5 cm) thick.

2

Make small balls of clay in different colors and press them into the flat piece of clay using the rolling pin.

3

Using the clay tools or knife, cut out an egg shape, making sure you smooth down the edges.

4

Press a brooch pin into the back of the clay egg.

5

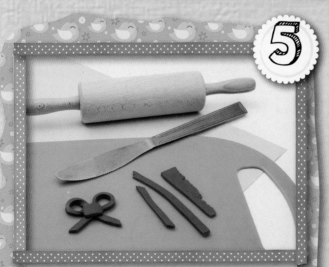

Make a clay bow and press it onto the middle of the egg. Bake the clay as instructed on the packet so that it hardens and is ready to wear.

Pin the badge to the front of a folded piece of card stock to make an Easter card that doubles up as a gift!

Crêpe paper chicken hanging

These clucking chickens will hang anywhere, but if you put them near an open window you will see their feathers rustle in the wind!

You will need:

- A paper plate
- Orange, yellow, and red card stock
- Scissors
- A glue stick
- Yellow and green crêpe paper
- Adhesive tape
- Googly eyes
- A stapler

1

Make two feet from the orange card stock and sandwich them in between a folded paper plate. Glue the plate down to stick them firmly into place.

2

Cut a wavy shape out of red card stock to make the chicken's comb. Glue this to the folded edge of the paper plate.

3

Cut two wing shapes out of yellow card stock.

4

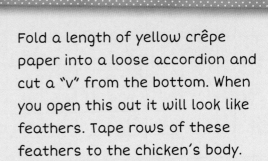

Fold a length of yellow crêpe paper into a loose accordion and cut a "v" from the bottom. When you open this out it will look like feathers. Tape rows of these feathers to the chicken's body.

5

Stick the wings onto the body and make an orange beak to go underneath the comb. Finally glue on some googly eyes and staple a strip of green crêpe paper to the top so your chicken can hang up.

Make some chicks in the same way but use smaller paper plates instead. Remember, chicks don't have a comb, so you won't need to make one for them

Websites

For web resources related to the subject of this book, go to: **www.windmillbooks.com/weblinks** and select this book's title.

Glossary

bonnet a type of hat, often decorated with flowers

comb the wavy crest on the head of a chicken

confetti tiny pieces of colored paper

feathery covered in feathers

festivities festive activities, or celebrations

meadow a field of grass, often used to graze animals on

recycle to remake something into something else

skip to move along with light, hopping steps

Index